PICTURES AND THEIR STORIES

The author wishes to express his gratitude
to Thomas Thornton, Kimberly Haller and
Frances Uckermann for their support.

Published in 1992 by Fromm International Publishing Corporation

Printed in Iceland

First U.S. Edition

Art Direction and Design: Susanne Adrian
Produced by Michael Josefowicz for Red Ink Productions, Inc.

Library of Congress Cataloging-in-Publication Data
Sahihi, Ashkan.
    Pictures and their stories / Ashkan Sahihi. — 1st U.S. ed.
    p. cm.
    ISBN 0-88064-141-X
    1. Celebrities—Portraits. I. Title
    TR681.F3S24 1992
    779' .2'092—dc20   92—16654
                                          CIP

PICTURES AND THEIR STORIES

ASHKAN SAHIHI

Fromm International Publishing Corporation
New York

For
the Butterfly
the Pegasus and
the Pink Monkey Bird

Contents

Publisher's Note

Ashkan Sahihi was born in Iran, spent his youth and early adulthood in Iran and West Germany, and for the past several years has lived in New York. Such wide (and profound) exposure to different cultures doubtless gives him a unique perspective into human nature. Sahihi's multicultural background was certainly formative, but his remarkable perception and ability for penetrating interpretation are innate qualities. He is also a visual artist endowed with a distinct literary sensitivity.

As an artist, Sahihi is interested exclusively in portraits. When he talks about his work, he invariably tells stories about his shooting sessions that give us additional insights into what is depicted in the actual photographs. These stories—including their moments of enlightening gossip—are fundamental to Ashkan Sahihi's work. He must have always known instinctively that they point to the core of his creative effort, because since the beginning of his career he has kept an artistic journal in which he writes his observations and impressions following each shooting session.

These stories hint at Sahihi's relationship with his subjects. It is a relationship that seems almost erotic, demonstrating this artist's deeply personal approach to his work, and revealing that human beings are indeed his main preoccupation. Frequently on assignment for magazines and in the company of reporters, Sahihi has photographed people from all walks of life, from superstar to down-and-out, from head of state to pimp. Given his artistic *eros* and personal interests in movies, music, and literature, however, it was only natural that the subjects chosen for this book be personages who play an important role in our cultural life, whether the standard of importance was strictly popular, more personal, or both.

Yet the stories Ashkan Sahihi has to tell not only reveal one artist's particular sensibility; they are portraits in their own right. *Pictures and their Stories* not only shows us a representative sample of this photographer's work, but also his interpretation and judgment of a subject and a situation *before* they are transformed into an image. The narrations in *Pictures and their Stories* give us a look behind the scenes and provide us with the actual background the images contain.

The combination of the verbal and the visual lets us share not only *what* the artist himself sees, but also gives us a look at *how* he sees. The translation process from interpretation to visualization, which is Ashkan Sahihi's self-imposed task, is made almost palpable; and the viewer/reader is challenged to retrace the creative process.

The working title of this book had been *Portraits and Their Development.* By combining, in a manner of speaking, the artistic challenge *and* its visual realization, this book's concept somehow mirrors the paradox of the artistic photograph itself: for while the final, developed image is necessarily still, it is the sum of a great variety of components, many of which are components of movement. This paradox suggests that a photograph in itself can be a perfect work of art despite the genre's natural limitations, and, of course, every art *thrives* on its limitations, precisely because, one way or another, it is forced to transcend them. Just as words can create indelible images, so can a two-dimensional photograph convey what usually belongs in the domain of words: they can open up the dimensions of history, because the fleeting moment the photograph captures is a product of the past and contains the seeds of the future. It is the *artistic* photograph's particular accomplishment to capture the essential within the seemingly incidental. Ashkan Sahihi, in both words and images, has achieved exactly that.

T.T.

Mr. Kosinski

"Mr. Kosinski will be with you in a moment," the woman said and walked her Wagnerian stature away.

So they had decided to make us wait. Wait for "Mr. Kosinski," who finally stepped out to display himself as a tall man, yet leaving the impression of a gnome-like posture.

"Make yourselves comfortable," he gestured us to sit back down. A host in his own home, nonetheless all functions of defense on highest alert, he had a readiness to pull up his shoulders in order to cover his head.

His response to each and every question was a counterquestion, and his eyebrow would not go down.

I wish it had rained that day, but it didn't. I rolled my window way down the moment the cab dashed away from the entrance of the Hemisphere House.

Jerzy Kosinski is the author of *The Painted Bird*, in which he copes with his childhood experiences in his native country, war-torn Poland. Among his other books are *Pinball* and *The Hermit on 53rd Street*. Kosinski was also President of PEN American. He lived and worked in New York City until his suicide in the summer of 1991.

Jacek Wozniakowski

He carries himself with a sense of dignity that makes you think of God when he enters the space that you are in. I remember hearing my heartbeat while he looked at me through the lens that brought him even closer. It was the first and only time I told a man who was much older, far higher in his social standing, and whom I did not know at all, that I thought he was very beautiful. Highly embarrassed by my own remark, I pulled the camera back into my face to take some more pictures. Jacek Wozniakowski then told me that as a young man, a bullet had hit his face in combat. He was in a field hospital, still dizzy and drowsy, when another young soldier came over, pointed his finger close to the wound and said, "From now on you will be carrying this thing in your face. You will be very ugly for the rest of your life." Then he laughed and walked away.

Jacek Wozniakowski indeed believed that he was ugly the day I met him.

Jacek Wozniakowski teaches Art History at the Catholic University in Lublin. He is one of the founding members of Klub Intelgencji Katolickiej in Warsaw, as well as the so-called "Flying University" which helped Polish Solidarity gain public support. He was one of the chairmen of the Polish Writers Association, which was dissolved under martial law.

Quentin Crisp

Quentin Crisp wants to be "infinitely available" to the public, waiting to be approached, and he *is* available, as much as his age allows. We met for lunch. He avoided garlic, ate only a light chicken sandwich, and drank a beer (Heineken).

He had been taking antibiotics, since he had a bit of a cold. The combination made him tired and very calm. He fell asleep several times during the shoot and I had to keep waking him up.

Quentin Crisp's autobiography, *The Naked Civil Servant*, was made into a movie in which he was played by John Hurt. Some time after moving from England to the U.S., *Resident Alien*, a documentary on Quentin Crisp, was released. Quentin Crisp lives in New York City's Lower East Side.

Lakim Shabazz

What fascinated me about this young man was his anger. It was an anger that I have only seen young African-American men exude. It had a strong sense of alertness, a hypersensitivity that lets one only guess what hurt or pain must be behind it.

This picture came very naturally. We hardly talked. We tried different positions, gestures and shots, most of them strong. The moment he lifted his fist towards the lens, we knew we had it. Not as much in a (strictly) political but rather in a personal sense, this very moment felt like "brothers in arms."

Lakim Shabazz belongs to the New School of Rap artists, formed by the teachings of Islam and influenced by such leaders as Malcolm X, whose Muslim name he has taken on for himself. He believes in and preaches "awareness" of African-American issues.

Paul Auster

Paul is a person you believe, because he doesn't seem to have a reason to lie.

Paul is the type of man you could love as much as his wife does, but you could also see yourself divorcing him as his ex-wife did. Paul is the father you always wanted, could probably be the best uncle or brother in the world but the worst friend to himself.

Paul could be the man you see pulling himself through cities, eyes lost on the ground as if looking for a lost key and hands in his pockets as if looking for lost matches.

Every generation loses quite a few of its most brilliant children to the research on how far you can go. We should be thankful for those enduring and offering us insight into their research papers and files.

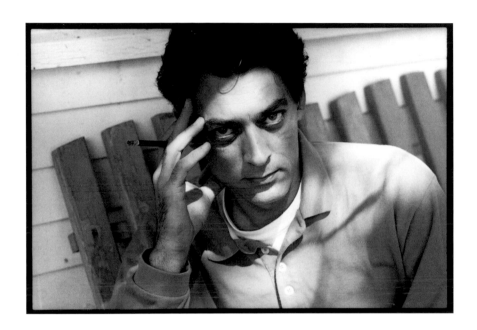

Paul Auster's publications include *The New York Trilogy (City of Glass, Ghost,* and *The Locked Room), Music of Chance,* and, in 1992, *Leviathan.* His work has been translated into eight languages. Paul Auster lives and works in Brooklyn, New York.

The Jesus and Mary Chain

They were fidgety and drank beer during the entire shoot, which had been going very well so far.

I asked them to hold or embrace each other. In his strong accent the shorter one said, "We don't do that. We are brothers, but we are not buddies," while the other one drank some more beer and looked away.

"Well, OK, then don't," and we kept shooting.

They complained they didn't like the music on the radio. I offered them Bowie, and the shorter one said, "We don't like Bowie," while the other one looked away and drank beer.

"Well, then go to hell," I thought, and I kept shooting.

The Jesus and Mary Chain are a hardcore band. They have released several albums, among them *Barbed Wire Kisses*, *Automatic*, and *Honey's Dead*.

Wendell B. Harris

If a fairy came down to Flint, Michigan, and told Wendell B. Harris he needed only clap three quick times to become whoever he wants to be, the world would have Orson Welles once again.

I like Wendell very much. In fact, I had a great time hanging out with him and we had a lot in common.

However, I think I once got him upset. Sitting in the front seat, being driven home for dinner, he turned slowly back to me. His deep voice exhaled Dunhill smoke. "Say, Ashkan, what should I do to get the cover of your magazine?" I could not resist and grinned back, "Die in a car accident."

Wendell B. Harris wrote, directed, and played the male lead in *Chameleon Street*. His whole family was involved in the movie, which won the Sundance Film Award. Harris lives and works in Flint, Michigan.

Schama

"Here I am," from across the tastefully decorated lobby. He stands tall. Nicely dressed, speaking in a formal business tone. He needs two (showing us with his fingers) more minutes, "Wait in my office."

The secretary opens his office in the attic, smaller and more personal than any other office I have ever seen. The Cambridge sun comes in massively and dustily through the round-topped windows. No modern city view, just a church tower displaying the time. No sounds except for footsteps just a few floors down on the sidewalk.

He sits down with us. "Ready," he says.

Any thought or idea creates and consumes energy. As much as its arrival rocks you back and forth, its birth feeds off you, makes you sweat and shrink. By the time it's explained, Schama is older, shorter, a little heavier and no longer well dressed at all. He even has a new hairdo. He is more likeable too.

Simon Schama is Mellon Professor in the Social Sciences and Senior Associate at the Center for European Studies at Harvard. He is the author of *Citizens: A Chronicle of the French Revolution*

and *Patriots and Liberators: Revolution of the Netherlands*. His latest book, *Dead Certainties*, is his first "experiment at narration." He lives with his wife and two children in Massachusetts.

Norman Loftis

He is tall. He is handsome. He has a baritone voice. He takes up space by his sheer presence. At the time I photographed him, he had not yet found a distributor for his movie *Small Time*. I wonder whether that might have been because other people, specifically men, were as intimidated by the basic signals he puts out as I was.

Norman Loftis's "no-budget" film *Small Time* is about a seventeen-year-old small-time criminal named Vince. The entire movie is shot in black-and-white and was mainly funded by Loftis himself. He lives in New York and teaches literature.

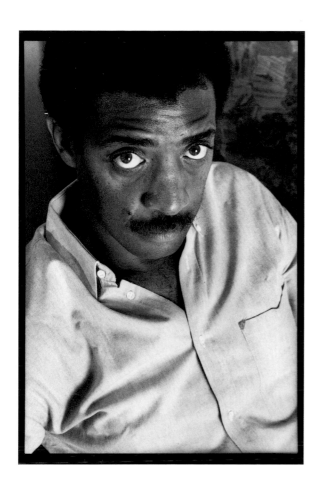

Philip Glass

People sometimes do not show up for shoots. They have another appointment or are simply too busy. When somebody whose work you have admired for years does that to you, you take it personally. Philip Glass had flown out to Houston, to the Grand Opera, and had forgotten about me. How could he? I was mad enough to pay for my own ticket to Houston and get everything set up through the wonderful press liaison at the opera to still get this portrait of Mr. Glass.

His jeans under his little belly, his hair unarranged as always, he stepped in through the stage door, putting away his reading glasses. He lightly hugged me. "What can I say?" his calm eyes and low voice asked me. I have never forgiven anybody so fast.

Philip Glass has created many compositions for opera, theatre, and film. They include *Einstein on the Beach, The Photographer, A Thousand Airplanes on the Roof, The Making of the Representative of Planet A,* and *Hydrogen Jukebox,* among others. Philip Glass lives and works in New York City.

The picture on the right shows him with Doris Lessing, author of the libretto for *The Making of the Representative of Planet A.*

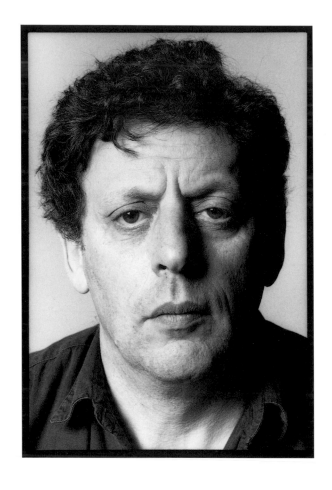

Kip

Kip talks fast. Kip talks very fast, because there is always so much to say, and the risk of being misunderstood, or not understood at all, is so big.

So he talks with his mouth, of course, but also his hands, his shoulders, and his elbows. He talks about "passion, anger and sexuality." While he explains what seems to be rocketing through his brain and guts at the same time, his entire physique is under a mild form of spasms that are almost exciting to watch.

He dances back and forth from you with little steps, and all his explanations, stories, and all his improv-philo-essays end not with a period, but with a look that quintessentializes the fear of being misunderstood once more.

Kip Hanrahan was born in 1954. He has been equally successful as a composer and a producer. His compositions include: *Desire Develops an Edge* (1983), *Day and Night of Blue Luck Inverted* (1987), and *Tenderness* (1990). As a producer he has worked closely with musicians such as Astor Piazola, releasing *Tango Zero Hour* in 1986 and *The Rough Dancer* in 1987. Kip Hanrahan lives and works in New York City.

This Is John Irving

This is John Irving. The right answer comes with a smile. I keep trying again and again to get through to him, but he has already made up his mind about his most photogenic pose.

I drove back from Long Island to New York City feeling shallow and disappointed with myself.

I am sure he would be very successful in any business.

John Irving wrote *The World According to Garp, A Prayer for Owen Meany,*

and many other novels. He lives and works in New York.

Charles Burnett

If you try to focus your eyes on "out of focus," a point where there is no object, no visual obstacle your eyes might cling to, you can see your own pictures. You can see very beautiful pictures, images and stories that you wish you could bring back with you to the "in focus" part of your life to show to other people.

If you try to focus your eyes on the "out of focus" too often, you might become a brilliant filmmaker or turn into a complete spacehead.

Charles is both. He is a director, the man who keeps a whole set under control, but ordering breakfast seemed be to such a difficult chore that I caught myself being tempted to help.

The evening I had the chance to see his beautiful movie *To Sleep with Anger*, which was shown to a packed theatre that applauded him for quite a while, he started his speech with an apology for having forgotten his dark suit.

Charles Burnett's first movie, *Killer of Sheep,* won an award at the 1981 Berlinale. His second movie, *To Sleep with Anger,* won at the annual Sundance Film Festival in Salt Lake City. It shows the encounters of a family with a long-lost mysterious friend, played by Danny Glover. Charles Burnett lives and works in Los Angeles.

Hector Bianciotti

Elegance and loneliness.

A heart that has been broken too often but has never given up believing in love and true beauty. Uprooted and replanted too often for one lifetime, still trying to grow and blossom. Passion that is not part of daily life infuses nightly dreams.

An old woman in a dark dress forcing herself through life and Paris. A writer whose pocket square and suit lining match.

How come those beaten worst keep their childhood eyes the longest?

Hector Bianciotti, an Argentinian citizen of Italian origin, lives in Paris. He published a play, several novels and short stories in Spanish. His first book written in French, *Sans la misérericorde du Christ* (1985), won the important French Prix Femina Award, as did *Le Traité des Saisons* and *L'amour n'est pas aimé*.

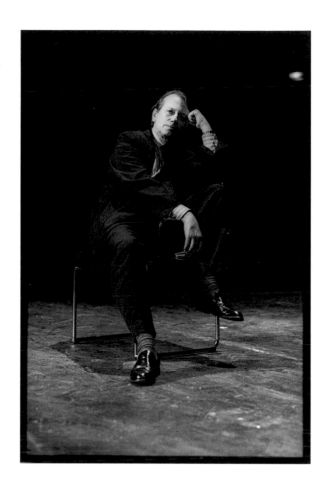

Hans

Why shave early at home when you can shave in the men's room of the United Nations? Why wear a conservative tie when you can put on your favorite one, the one you bought at a flea market traveling god-knows-where in the world? First and foremost, why walk around, look serious and not smile when the world is such a funny place? Well then, the world is a court and the king is the King, but the jester might be the ruler. So tuck in that tie, grab your razor, go for a stroll to the men's room. After all, the world is such a funny place.

Hans Janitschek was born in Vienna in 1934. After studying law in Austria and the U.S., he chose a career in journalism. He joined the Austrian Foreign Service in 1963 and served as Austria's Consul to the U.S. in New York for two years. Janitschek was elected Secretary General of the Socialist International in 1969, and was re-elected twice. He became a consultant to the U.N. in 1977 on such subjects as Palestine and Human Rights. Janitschek lives in New York City.

Woody Allen

After making us wait for six months, they made us wait a few more hours. We sat in our car, parked behind his location van on 49th Street. My suggestion to give us a few minutes with Allen, so we could get out of their way instead of following them from location to location, was finally taken seriously, somewhat too seriously. They gave me about seven minutes to shoot a cover, an opener, and, if possible, a few fillers for the layout. These seven minutes also included final light check and test polaroids. His personal assistant stood right behind me. Each and every time the strobe went off, she would say, her eyes locked on her watch, "Oh, it flashed! Are you done now?"

Woody Allen is a true auteur, with a long history of films in which he often appears as the male lead. Among them are *Stardust Memories*, *A Midsummer Night's Sex Comedy*, *Zelig*, *Crimes and Misdemeanors*, and *Shadows and Fog*. He won an Academy Award for *Annie Hall*.

K.R.S.-1

Hi-fi set and video equipment were overthroned by a giant-screen TV blasting out the latest MTV rap songs. Perfect to be included in a portrait shot. For the test polaroid, K.R.S. sat with his back to the fast, grainy video clip images. "That's scary," K.R.S. diagnosed the picture, "There are five brothers in this video clip but your polaroid shows six." He handed me the picture. He was right. Pointing at the screen, he went on, "That's scary, man. Too much modern technology wakes up ghosts. My stuff and your equipment . . . We can't use the TV in the picture . . . We can't!"

We didn't.

K.R.S.-1 is active as a recording artist and an educator. He experienced the hardships of being homeless as well as losing his friend D.J. Scott La Rock to street violence. The rapper's activites outside the studio include H.E.A.L. (Human Education Against Lies) to raise the standard of education, lectures at schools, and projects such as "Stop The Violence."

Joan Didion

Her fingers are desperately trying to get rid of all that energy. She wraps herself around the chair, her hands cling to whatever she can find. If she didn't speak so quietly she would probably yell. "Yes, you can move that seat," comes out rather unhappily. She repairs the damage as soon as possible. I don't even have the slightest chance to do it myself.

I was hot during the entire shoot, extremely hot. I was not sweating, but glowing inside to an uncomfortable degree.

These photographs mean a lot to me, which is fair, because I lost about four pounds taking them.

Joan Didion's literary-political reportage includes a number of books, such as *White Album*, *Miami*, and *Salvador*. She and her husband John Gregory Dunne live and work in New York City.

James Bond III

There is something incredibly cute about James Bond III, his name, his chubbiness, his whole mannerism.

Whenever I take final test polaroids I take two, one for myself and one for the person photographed. James Bond III looked at both of them for a few minutes, because he couldn't decide in which one he looked better.

I finally gave up and he kept both.

James Bond III directed, wrote, and played the male lead in his first film, *Deaf by Temptation*, at the age of 24. He began acting when he was eight, playing young James Baldwin in a movie called *Go Tell the Mountains*.

Ruth Rubin

She moves quickly. She talks quickly. Ruth is like quicksilver. You must be fast to follow her. She has many stories to tell, little songs to hum, and she flirts all the time.

Focusing was incredibly hard, and setting up flash equipment would have bored her too much. I used high-speed film for high-speed Ruth.

Ruth Rubin is one of the last singers who grew up within the Yiddish musical tradition, which makes her an authority on translating and fully interpreting Yiddish texts. Her friendship and creative exchange with Pete Seeger is as much a part of her life as are projects with other contemporary musicians dedicated to Jewish music. Her latest recording is available on the sampler *The Heimliche Groove*. She lives and works in New York City.

The Hudlin Brothers

Photographing them was quite a thrill. The nonverbal choreography between them was strongly interactive and seemed completely natural. They seemed aware of the frame, me, and definitely of each other.

The Hudlin Brothers make their own movies. Reginald directs, and Warrington produces. Inspired by Spike Lee, they became motivated to find the two and a half million dollars it took to shoot *House Party,* one of the biggest successes of 1990.

Reich

This week I will photograph Steve Reich, whose work I admire tremendously. I wonder how excited or nervous I will be? To create pieces of art within one's passion that are as dense, strong and beautiful as his compositions must be nirvana. I have only seen him on stage, I wonder what he is like as a person. (Reich in German means "empire" as a noun and "rich" as an adjective.)

Reich is concerned about Louis Farrakhan being part of this book. Reich's office requested to see my writing about Farrakhan before confirming the shoot. I refused to do so, I consider it inappropriate. They said they would get back to me. I am upset and I don't want to think about it right now.

Today I photographed Steve Reich.

I was nervous as hell. To meet somebody whose work you admire so much means a lot, but to be allowed into the room where "99.9% of the works" are composed is pretty breathtaking. I had to talk quietly and slowly, concerned my voice would become high-pitched by itself. There were a couple of books, records, and CDs that I would have loved to look at, but, interestingly enough, for the portrait shot I couldn't help but totally concentrate on his face. I felt it was definitely strong enough to hold a frame by itself. It contained enough information within itself that the picture didn't need all the things the room would have added. There is hardly any photograph that I have taken so much just for myself. I still was very nervous. We only used two rolls of 120 film (12 frames each) but I feel as if I had carried stones all day. It is 9:15 PM, and I am dying to see my films tomorrow.

I got the contact sheets. The pictures are good, but I wish I hadn't been that nervous. Biggest mistake: his face is too strong for any kind of background, I should have used a backdrop. I am very unhappy with myself.

Steve Reich is one of the most outstanding minimalist composers in today's music scene. He has experimented with music for decades. His work includes *It's Gonna Rain* (1965), pieces for big ensembles, *Music for 18 Musicians* (1978), and, lately, collaborations with musicians such as Pat Metheny. Steve Reich lives and works in New York City.

Joel Carmichael

Some apartments seem to be somewhere other than the city they are actually in. Roland Topor's fascinating book *The Tenant* was made into one of my all-time favorite movies by Roman Polanski. One of the characters in the story, which takes place in Paris, is the landlord, a very evil character who lives with his housekeeper.

Alone with a woman I had wrongly assumed to be Joel Carmichael's housekeeper, I was waiting for him to arrive. I could not help but think that this was the way I imagined the landlord's apartment to look in Paris, a space in which time had a different feel. Finally meeting Joel Carmichael, I was even more surprised to see that he and the actor playing the landlord resemble each other very much. Although Joel Carmichael is far from evil—he is a kind, polite and interesting person—I was intimidated by this resemblance and think it shows in the pictures.

Joel Carmichael is a respected expert on the history of Russia and the Soviet Union, as well as the origins of Christianity. His book *The Death of Jesus* was translated into nine languages. Carmichael holds a B.A. and an M.A. from Oxford University, and has translated works by Tolstoy and Aidanov. His most recent book is *The Satanizing of the Jews: Origins and Development of Mystical Anti-Semitism* (1992).

The Jungle Brothers

I had planned to photograph them each individually and then combine the photographs in one picture, like a puzzle. Strong and solid, they seemed very much like a unit with its own code. It became evident that only a group picture would do to illustrate the relationship within this group.

The Jungle Brothers are rappers who put emphasis on the historical and cultural awareness of the African American community. The motif "Africa" is important to them and is reflected in their music, in songs such as Acknowledge Your History.

Peter Wortsman

The pictures Peter has in his mind are very similar to those I like, so certain inhibitions fell faster. He was vivid in expressing what he imagined and suggestions from my side seemed to be very much to his fancy. One summer's Saturday afternoon we ended up in Manhattan's Meat Packing District. The heat was deadly enough to keep most of the johns away who come for the transvestites. We played like children and it felt as if we were in somebody else's living room. The heat and the smell didn't keep us from trying more and more things, finding yet another fascinatingly chipped wall or harsh play of light.

Evidently this kind of excitement leads to a disrespect for authorities, as excitements tend to do in general. We forgot to care about time. We both were late for appointments, we just played.

Peter Wortsman's first book of fiction, *A Modern Way To Die*, was published in 1992. Previously, he published several short stories that were also translated for European magazines. His own work as a translator includes Robert Musil's *Posthumous Papers of a Living Author*. Peter Wortsman lives in New York City with his wife and child.

Billy Wilder/Walter Matthau

On the one hand, Wilder wanted to be in the limelight and to be photographed. On the other hand, he has been calling the shots for so many years, and on so many star-studded sets, that it seemed hard for him to have some kid photographer with a ponytail telling him what to do. It needed tender pushiness not to be sent away with only the shot which he had arranged and I didn't like.

Finally they came, and he even went out of his way to say (to the reporter, not me) that he liked the location. But now, of course, Wilder would not sit still.

Matthau, meanwhile, seemed more relaxed. He came, paid a debt to Wilder from a bet they had made the day before, sat quietly during the entire shoot, and then, without complaint, drove Wilder home.

Billy Wilder's and Walter Matthau's careers are closely knit. Wilder, the only director with five Academy Awards, left Germany escaping from the Nazis. He started out writing screenplays for Ernst Lubitsch in Hollywood until he began directing himself. His expertise, combined with Walter Matthau's unforgettable face and incredible comedic abilities, made possible such cinematic masterpieces as *Fortune Cookie*. They are still close friends and both live and work in Los Angeles.

Charles "Honi" Coles

Dignity that is created in the head turns into arrogance.

Dignity that is rooted in the heart grows into the elegance with which Charles "Honi" Coles carries himself.

Charles "Honi" Coles is one of the great American tap dancers, even though he has never had lessons. He worked with such greats as Basie, Ellington, and Waller in the '30s and '40s. He danced on Broadway in *Gentlemen Prefer Blondes* and at the Apollo. For *My One and Only* he won a Tony Award. Having had a stroke that left him unable to dance, he now concentrates on acting and working with directors such as Robert Wilson.

J. F. Federspiel

He came in a rush, drank his coffee in a rush, and left after a few rolls of film. I had to sit down to catch my breath.

I wonder how Federspiel likes these pictures. I do. He watches the world pass by, trying to lean away from it all, out of the picture, trying to make himself less present.

J. F. Federspiel was born in Zurich, but has spent much of his life in Paris, Munich, Berlin, and New York. His home country has presented him various awards, including the Literary Award of the City of Zurich, and the Basel Literary Award. His latest novel is *Laura's Skin*. Today he lives in Zurich.

O. Winston Link

I felt pressured to photograph him with the same dedication to technical questions and big equipment that are typical of his work. It took me a while to realize that it was I who had set up that trap for myself. Of course, two photographers on their first encounter are catty beyond belief, but once we had sniffed each other out, guards were let down and equipment disappeared. Instead, the peaceful upstate sunlight pushed in and helped me take my favorite picture of "Winnie."

O. Winston Link combined his love for steam locomotives with his photographic skills to document the closing of an era in the late fifties, and through his efforts created photographic masterpieces. He lives in upstate New York and owns his own steam engine.

Farrakhan

". . . and remember, the Minister will address you first with 'Salamulaleik.' You then will answer 'Assalamulaleik,'" the person in charge of dealing with the press reminded us once more the day before our meeting with Minister Louis Farrakhan.

The next morning, the reporter was as nervous as they wanted him to be. We arrived at Farrakhan's house too early and decided to park the car a few blocks away. In the car the reporter kept rehearsing "Salamulaleik"—"Assalamulaleik."

As the gate opened, the guards waved invitingly at us and didn't care at all to check the car or my equipment. The front door was opened by the friendly housekeeper, who in a splendid early-morning mood remembered seeing me at The Nation's Congress in D.C.

We were taken through the bright, big white room to a smaller adjoining room where the reporter was happy to try "Assalamulaleik" one last time before "He" arrived.

He arrived, striding down the stairs. Quiet, modest steps. A well-groomed, clean-shaven gentleman at the best age a gentleman can be looked openly at both of us, extended his hand. *Everything* was well-orchestrated. In a well-modulated voice he asked, "How do you do, gentlemen?"

Minister Louis Farrakhan became the leader of The Nation of Islam after Elijah Mohammed's death. He lives in the Hyde Park District of Chicago, where the headquarters of The Nation is based.

Jiri Georg Dokoupil

I missed a very good picture of Georg that I could have taken after his opening at the Robert Miller Gallery: a small crowd was taken to a go-go bar. Between topless dancers, half-naked waitresses, and his confused artsy friends, Georg went to get his shoes polished by the beautiful shoeshine girl. Sitting on the throne, he held on tightly to the neck of his beer bottle, grinning happily at all his friends.

Jiri Georg Dokoupil was born in Krnov, Czechoslovakia, in 1954. He studied art in Germany and New York and has worked as a guest teacher in Germany and Spain. He lives and paints in Germany, Spain, and New York City. Dokoupil is married and has one child.

John

He had been sick for a while, just moved into his new place, and had to grow a beard for a movie role. Knowing we both had trips ahead of us, he agreed to be photographed although he was not fully recovered yet, and despite the inconvenience of moving and not liking himself unshaven.

"Up here," I hear him say, as he stands at the top of the stairs, his TV set humming in the background. Saturday, rainy, New York City. A man (unshaven) and his sports broadcast.

He mumbles some half-hearted explanation which I can't hear, and then, "I am watching the game." Off he goes, right back to his futon on the floor, positioned for perfect viewing pleasure of the color TV, the only other piece of furniture in the room.

"No kidding," I think. Setting up my equipment, I decide to have John stay (or lie) exactly where he is.

"All the girls I told I was shooting you today asked me to say hello."

"Oh yeah," he runs his big hand through his semibeard. I start shooting. He turns back to the game but leaves enough attention for me. He can still react and interact, but we hardly talk. Only once there is an exchange. We talk about cigarettes. Handy, we smoke the same brand. I hardly interrupt the shooting. I signal him to get his attention or to make a change of position, trying not to disturb his listening to the sportscaster at the same time. He seems fine, comfortable enough. I decide to ask, "Are you OK?" I expose my face from behind the camera. John looks at me, "Yeah, of course. I get to lie here, watch the game, and at the same time you make me famous."

John Lurie records and performs with his band The Lounge Lizards. He has written several movie scores for Jim Jarmusch, with whom he started his movie career as an actor (*Stranger than Paradise, Down by Law*). John Lurie lives and works in New York.

Dorothea Tanning

After some initial shyness on both sides, after some "ground-and-code testing," it turned more into a date. We listened to *Spanish Sketches* again and again. Once the time had come for homemade pie and coffee, we were already making fun of shrinks. Toward evening she showed me the old manual typewriter she had written her memoirs on, even allowed me to photograph the instrument. Shortly before I left, she took me to the bookshelf in the bedroom, fingered between two books, and pulled out an old black-and-white photograph. "A snapshot a friend of Max's and mine took years ago when I was young and beautiful." An 8 x 10 photograph, its colors already changing into the shades of old book pages, her beautiful young face in a very, very grainy close-up. Full bleed, no margin. I moved the embossed copyright against the light so I could read: Man Ray.

Dorothea Tanning's autobiography, *Birthday*, was published on her 80th birthday. *Birthday* is also the title Max Ernst gave the self-portrait she was working on when they met for the first time. Max Ernst and Dorothea Tanning lived together until Ernst died in 1976. Dorothea Tanning lives, paints, and writes in New York City.

Francesco Clemente

I have a hard time putting into words what my problem with Clemente is. He puts out mixed messages. His paintings and what he says about his art and himself strongly suggest spirituality, yet in his encounters with people he seems to see through some kind of class bias, or hierarchy. He paints and talks about birth and death and his modest attempt to understand life better, but he didn't even give me the chance to introduce my assistant to him before the shooting. He turned away after shaking hands with me, as if she hadn't been there. I thought that was rude, and a contradiction to the way he presents himself through his art, in interviews and in photographs.

He didn't leave any doubt that he was doing us a favor by sharing his time and fame with us. But that is understood anyway, there is no need for emphasis. We already know that every time a famous person gives an interview or grants a portrait session, they give away a slice of their fame in exchange for possible media attention. What is the point in making people actually feel it?

Francesco Clemente was born in Naples, Italy, in 1952. He is considered one of the strongest influences in figurative painting, with psychoanalysis and Far Eastern philosophy as his main sources. He travels back and forth between Madras, India, and New York City, where he has had his studio since 1983.

Falco

What happens when your star starts fading? When you are still hungry for a lot more but it doesn't keep comin' no more? You get out of breath, you get out of sync.

The faster your heart beats the less seems to happen.

You don't excite anymore, anyone, not even yourself, but still you are constantly "on" because you need it and "one never knows........!"

Falco or "Hansi," as his friends call him, had several number-one hits on the European and American charts, among them *Der Kommissar* and *Amadeus*. Falco lives in Vienna, Austria.

Jerry Lee Lewis

A former photo editor of a New York magazine calls these assignments "combat photography." Just a few minutes, no briefing, late at night, everybody slightly exhausted. Now, of course, I think it was funny, but I didn't until the film was developed. Indeed, only one frame is good enough to be shown. In the others, the strain of all of the shoots and interviews he had done that day shows on his face even more strongly than it does in this one.

Jerry Lee Lewis, nicknamed "The Killer," is after Elvis Presley the most important symbol of American rock 'n' roll. Hollywood made Lewis's life into a movie, Great Balls Of Fire, named after his famous song. Jerry Lee Lewis lives in Memphis, Tennessee.

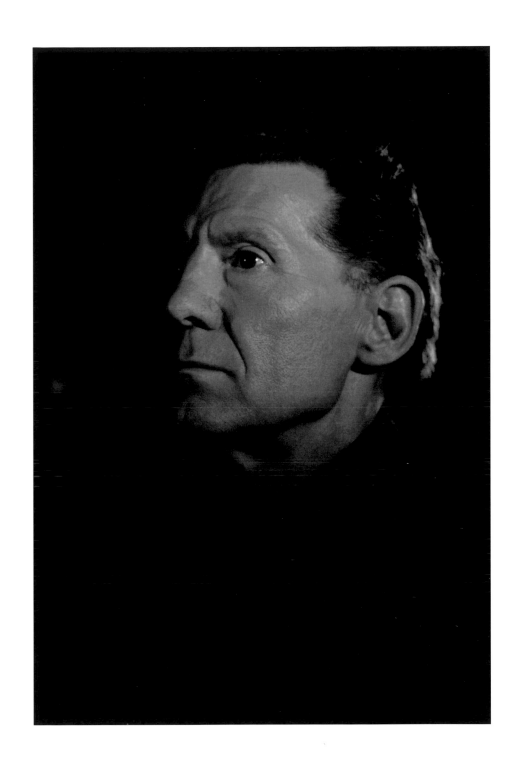

Big Daddy Kane

It was the height of his popularity, his ego not adjusting well at all. Who to trust? Any change or repositioning that I would ask him for, he would first shoot a wry look over to his agent. Only his OK counted.

Everything on him was brand-new. His leather jacket, his clothing, his car radio. The only thing he said repeatedly was, "Photograph me with my car."

(. . . I hate cliché photographs of musicians with their cars.)

Big Daddy Kane is a rapper from the Bedford Stuyvesant neighborhood in Brooklyn. He started making a name for himself as a songwriter for Kurtis Blow, Rick James and many others. His own debut as a recording artist was an album called *Long Live the Kane*, in 1987. Several albums have followed, the latest being *Prince of Darkness*, in 1991.

Arnulf Rainer

The fearful European in the disguise of an artist wanted to be portrayed at places in our city where terrible things have happened, where misery frequently stays overnight. Once we got him there, he was very scared and very much in a hurry to leave.

Arnulf Rainer's large-scale black-and-white photographs, on which he paints, have become Austria's number-one art export. In New York his work has been exhibited at the Guggenheim Museum in a one-man show. Arnulf Rainer lives and works in Austria.

Nick

If the interaction of shooting a portrait were compared to ballroom dancing, I would say that Nick was leading that day, and it was a pleasure to follow him.

The outcome of these pictures must be credited to Nick's professionality and his ability to concentrate in spite of all the people at this shoot: Makeup, Assistant, Second Assistant, Editor, Record Company, . . . and so on. Too many people tend to make shoots impersonal, and consequently it is harder to concentrate, for those photographed as well as the photographer.

I guess that is what a strong stage personality is about, not to be intimidated by people watching you perform. Nick seemed able to detach himself very well from all the commotion and noise around us. Once in a while, he would step off the backdrop and away from the lights to down a giant café au lait, smoke a cigarette, and be ready to continue the session.

Nick Cave is an Australian musician who started his career in 1982 with his first band, The Birthday Party. His second band, The Bad Seeds, was formed in 1984 and has released six albums so far. Nick Cave published his first novel, *The Ass Saw the Angel*, in 1989.

Ilma Rakusa

I was impressed by her. It took a deep breath to approach her. I was very much aware of my intrusion.

I asked if she would agree to being photographed. While I was explaining that her publisher had assigned me to portray her, she looked as if she could not hear me or understand me at all, like a movie in a foreign tongue, with the sound off. Then she answered, "Yes".

We took these pictures, and I had never before seen a woman who has such beauty and authority with her lipstick smudged.

Ilma Rakusa studied Slavic and Romanic languages and literatures. Her field of expertise is Russian literature. She is also actively involved in the bi-lingual literary magazine *Parkett*. She has published several volumes of stories. Ilma Rakusa lives and works in Switzerland.

Jayne Anne Phillips

The more you know and like a person's work, the harder it seems to be to photograph him or her. I don't really know why that is, maybe because of a false sense of intimacy from which you feel you should detach yourself, maybe because of the added pressure of wanting to come up with a picture that is as strong as his or her work.

I was very nervous before meeting Jayne Anne Phillips in Boston, and, to make things worse, she had forgotten that we were coming. We waited in the cold on her porch for about an hour before giving up. When we finally met up with her, it was too dark to photograph and my stomach was bothering me with nervous spasms.

I came back around 9:00 the next morning for the portraits, having had to postpone my next shoot in New York, which made my schedule even tighter. There were so many things that I would have liked to ask her, but the time pressure, the nervousness, and maybe also some overpoliteness on my side forbade me from doing so. The evening before, she had mentioned that every day from 9:00-12:00 is reserved for her writing. I felt guilty for keeping her from her work.

These pictures are not what I wanted them to be. I was numb on my way to the airport and during the flight back. It wasn't until I was in the cab that took me home from LaGuardia Airport that I finally wept.

Jayne Anne Philips made her debut with a collection of stories called *Black Tickets*. Her first novel, *Machine Dreams* (1984), was highly acclaimed and was followed by a second collection of short stories in 1987, *Fast Lanes*. Jayne Anne Philips lives near Boston with her husband and two sons.

Illeana Sonnabend

An ex-girlfriend of mine would hardly talk whenever she wanted to drive me up the wall. She would just look at me as if I were stupid. Finally, when she knew she was in the stronger position, she would smile slyly.

After two rolls of film that went by with hardly a word spoken, and with my disappointment mounting, Illeana smiled at me.

Illeana Sonnabend and her gallery have been on the forefront of the New York art scene for many decades. She has had great influence on art by discovering and exhibiting important new artists as well as entire trends and movements. She helped set the stage for the pop-art era and today represents artists Jeff Koons and Ashley Bickerton.

A Tribe Called Quest

The latest charts had come in. Another rap band was seemingly doing too well, getting to be hotter than they currently were. The frantic pace of a new video production surrounded them. They had a hard time concentrating. They kept whispering back and forth, hardly relating to the camera, and were very detached from what was happening around them, putting out vibes that were getting to me too. "Guys, relax. Show some love," something I usually would not say. They looked up, stopped fidgeting, and almost immediately sank into each other.

"Thank you," I said.

A Tribe Called Quest are part of the latest generation of Rap artists. They describe and rap about subjects that are representative of their generation. Their issues are often motherland Africa and spirituality, but also pure fun.

Hans Wollschläger

It is very hard for most people to look straight at a camera for a long period of time. Everybody knows what a camera is, and how it can be used and abused. Very few people can detach themselves enough from this concern to remain as directly concentrated as Hans Wollschläger did. The intensity of his concentration reminded me of Klaus Kinski, whose rawness in acting I have always liked.

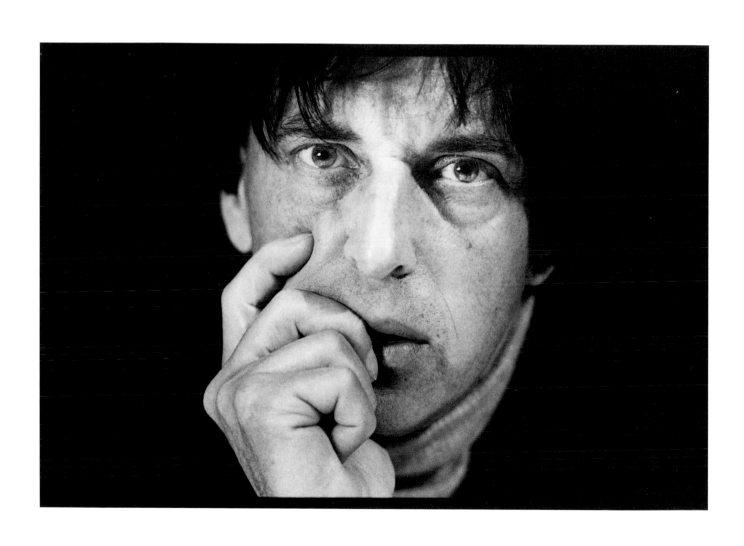

Hans Wollschläger became famous through his new German translation of James Joyce's *Ulysses*. He also champions other writers' work, such as Karl Kraus's œuvre. Hans Wollschläger's own literary output includes the novel *Herzflattern*, which is only available in German, since he expressly prohibited its translation into other languages. He lives in Germany.

John Cage

In the middle of the shoot, John Cage made his housekeeper bring him a pair of scissors. He started cutting the browning tips of the plant on the left side behind him. He trimmed with such loving care and dedication that I did not know how to recapture his attention to continue the shoot. "Sir . . . Sir . . . Mr. Cage," I forced myself to say, breaking his concentration. He mumbled some explanation about the plant, then, out of the blue, he laughed out loud very happily.

John Cage has been best known as a composer from the days of 1938 *Bacchanale* through to the recent *Europeras 3+4,* but he has also been heavily involved in most other media. He is the author of *Silence* (1961) and *X* (1963). In the graphics field, he created *Not Wanting to Say Anything Bad About Marcel* (1969), and more recently *The New River Watercolors Show* (1990). John Cage is a member of the American Academy of Arts and Sciences as well as the Academy of Arts and Letters. He lives and works in New York City.

Don Byron

He didn't want to. He didn't want to be photographed ("I have got press pictures.") Not in his apartment ("I am just moving.") Not in his kitchen ("Bad vibes in here man, definitely bad vibes.") Not in his bedroom ("Moving makes a mess.") All that made him complicated yet more likeable.

He is not a pro who has been photographed a million times, who knows his better side, and knows which room has the most photogenic light.

Don Byron is one of today's best jazz clarinetists. He plays with different musicians, such as John Zorn and Marc Ribot, but has dedicated a major part of his effort to Klezmerer music (Yiddish big-band folk music). His latest work, *Tuskegee Experiment*, released in 1992, was a collaboration with various artists highlighting his role as a band leader and composer.

Rev. Al Sharpton

After about two hours, we finally gave up. He was not going to show up for the shoot. Tired, I went out for dinner, losing my hope that I would still get to photograph him before the deadline. Three days later I spotted him at a convention of The Nation of Islam in Washington, D.C., where I had been sent to photograph Minister Louis Farrakhan. I approached him, got his hotel phone number, and called the next day to schedule an interview and photoshoot.

"Reverend Sharpton? Can we meet before you leave?"

"Yeah. Yeah, we can. Tomorrow, what about tomorrow?"

"Tomorrow is fine. Where and when?"

"Here in my hotel. 1 o'clock. Wanna have lunch together?"

"Perfect. Tomorrow. Lunch!"

"You pay!"

This photograph was taken after lunch.

Al Sharpton was born in the Brownsville section of Brooklyn in 1955, where, at age 4, he became a boy preacher of the Pentecostal Faith. He toured with Mahalia Jackson at age 11 and was a youth pastor until he was 18. In 1971 he formed The National Youth Movement, whose mission was to eradicate drugs from the black neighborhoods. Rev. Sharpton gained high public visibility in connection with the Tawana Brawley case, in which a black teenager claimed that she had been kidnapped and sexually assaulted by a gang of whites; the charge was dismissed as fraudulent.

Elliott Sharp

A young actress I knew used to clip a huge pink bowtie to her waist, hoping to distract people's attention from her big bosom. It never worked.

To pretend that Elliott's lips are not the first thing one's attention is drawn to would be hypocritical. In spite of his esthetically divine head, his strong eyes, and a nose from which some makeup artist should make a cast, Elliott's lips keep everybody in awe for the first moments, till mother's voice echoes way in the back, "Don't stare."

Elliott Sharp, the composer/multi-instrumentalist, is the band leader of three different groups (Carbon, Terraplane, and Bootstrappers) and also performs with several cooperative music groups, such as Sync. Sharp has performed improvised music since 1969 and has collaborated with ensembles in New York City since 1979. He received a National Endowment for the Arts Award for composition in 1988/89. He founded his own record company, Zoar, in 1977, to release not only his own music but also other artists' work. Sharp lives and works in New York City.

Cubby

His apartment smelled of incense. "You don't mind the music?" Of course I don't, some brass ensemble mixing with the solemn fragrance and the rather dim light in his neat, orderly space. He is tall, pale, slightly bent forward. "Being a romantic all your life is very hard," he warns me, and I know what he means. He is patient, kind, beautiful, and extremely concentrated while we work. Yet I am very relieved when I am done and can leave this private island in the old-people part of L.A. "My work exhausts me, after I wrote 'Tralala' I was sick in bed for two weeks."

Sitting in the cab I remember his bed standing next to his desk, a paisley pillow on a cozy, mustard-yellow comforter. I remember the Buddah statue, the rose petals strewn around it, and I know what he means.

Hubert Selby, Jr. or "Cubby," as he likes to be called by friends, is the author of the short story collection *Song of the Silent Snow* and several novels, among them *Requiem for a Dream*, *The Demon*, *The Room*, and *Last Exit to Brooklyn*, of which "Tralala" is a part. Hubert Selby, Jr. lives and works in Los Angeles.